I0075215

REAL ESTATE INVESTING 101

HOW YOU CAN GO FROM BROKE TO 7 FIGURES IN FIVE SIMPLE STEPS

Jiries Dawaher

Real Estate Investing 101

Copyright © 2022 by Jiries Dawaher.

All rights reserved. Printed in the United States of America. No part of this book may be used or reproduced in any manner whatsoever without written permission except in the case of brief quotations embodied in references, articles, or reviews.

S EDITION

For information contact:

🌐 www.jiriesd.com
📷 JiriesD
📘 Jiries Dawaher
▶️ Jiries Dawaher

Table of Contents

CHAPTER ONE

THE "BEFORE" IMAGE

© 2022 www.jiriesd.com | All rights reserved

I n 2012, I was driving someone else's 1992 champagne-colored Chevy Lumina, running on empty—literally in the case of the car, but even more so financially. I was barely scraping by and wasn't sure how things could get any worse.

I was about to find out.

As I pulled up to my rundown apartment, I was in for the shock of a lifetime. It felt like someone had punched me as hard as they could right in the gut. Someone had broken into my dingy little rental and stolen what little I had.

With less than ten dollars in my bank account, I drove to the Shell station in Pleasant Ridge, a suburb of Cincinnati, put five dollars' worth of gas in the car, and just started crying.

It was about as low a moment as I've ever experienced, and I wouldn't wish it on anyone.

If someone had told me then that within five years, I'd be making $11,000 a month in passive income, I would have given them a funny look and kept on walking.

If someone had told me that within eight years, I'd have over $2.6 million in equity growing at ten percent a year, I would have backed away slowly and wondered what they were smoking.

And if someone had told me that ten years later, I'd be writing a book to help *other* people learn how to make passive income and transform their lives, I would have laughed—probably a little hysterically—in their face.

© 2022 www.jiriesd.com | All rights reserved

But the truth is that after hitting rock bottom, things started to turn around. I got into real estate investing (I'll tell you exactly how a little later in the book) and gradually, I built a portfolio that is now worth more than $30 million ($7 million in apartments and $25 million in hotels)

I want to make it clear that this wasn't a get-rich-quick scheme. I worked hard, I made plenty of mistakes, and I had more than my share of ups and downs. Passive income is great, but it takes a lot of active hustle to get there. Over time, though, I figured things out, gained confidence, and realized I'd found my calling.

Maybe it will be your calling too.

Over the past decade, a clear five-step process to success in real estate has revealed itself:

1. Decide you're going to do this business and follow this process
2. Surround yourself with people who are where you want to be
3. Do your research
4. Choose your strategy
5. Take action

In this short book, I've mapped out what I've learned over the past decade so that you can avoid my mistakes and benefit from my learning. Hopefully, by sharing my experience, I can help make your journey to success faster and easier than mine.

Use this book to write in and take notes, share it with others, and review it regularly.

This is your field manual for making millions. Use it wisely.

CHAPTER TWO

HOW IT STARTED

I come from very humble beginnings. My parents came to America from Jordan in 1978 and settled in Youngstown, Ohio, where I was born. Youngstown is a Midwestern city just southeast of Cleveland, Ohio. It used to be a center of steel production, but the town fell into decline in the 1970s, just as my family was establishing its roots.

My dad was a hard worker, sometimes working two or three jobs, and rarely had time to spend with his family. Despite working hard, though, he only made eight or nine dollars an hour. During my childhood, it was normal to see Dad go from one job to the next making sure we had food, a roof over our heads, and safety and security. We had everything we needed but rarely anything extra. One year, my parents bought me a Nintendo 64, which was hard to get at the time—and I did not take that for granted.

Because we were at the poverty level, I was on a free lunch program throughout school. Sheepishly, I'd make my way to the end of the lunch line every day so that no one could see my name getting checked off the clipboard. Even at a very young age, I knew that I didn't want to be poor forever.

The smart thing would have been to work hard in school, get a scholarship to college, and use my education to land a secure, high-paying job. Unfortunately, I was a lousy student.

Although I excelled in business and marketing classes in high school, I made up for them with abysmal grades in everything else. My GPA was 1.53,

© 2022 www.jiriesd.com | All rights reserved

and I graduated—barely—311th out of a class of 320 kids.

When I told my guidance counselor that I wanted to go to college, he managed to not laugh at me and asked if I had any "more realistic" expectations. It was pretty clear that college was off the table. Later that day, I spoke to a recruiter for the military and signed up to join the Army.

While my reasons for joining the military weren't particularly noble or even very well thought out, the Army ended up being a great experience. I became a lot more self-disciplined and I learned a trade—I become a helicopter and a diesel mechanic.

Most importantly, I learned that I wasn't "stupid." High school hadn't been a great fit for me, and I'd never excelled academically. Here in the real world, though, I realized I was capable of learning, and learning quickly. I was good at the hands-on stuff, and I pushed myself in ways I'd never pushed myself before. I ended up graduating second in my helicopter mechanic class.

Later, after leaving the Army, I went into the National Guard, where I volunteered to go on all the missions I could—two weeks here, two weeks there, three weeks somewhere else—because it paid very well. I had a series of low-level, part-time jobs, and relied on the National Guard to help me make ends meet.

In 2003, I was idling at a stop light and noticed a bumper sticker on the back of a shiny new Saab that said, "Want wallet weight gain?" with a phone number.

I thought to myself, "Heck yeah, I want wallet weight gain. Sign me up!"

I called the number on the bumper sticker and talked to a woman who shared some info on a company called Excel Communications that sold long-distance phone service. Excel is a now-defunct multi-level marketing (MLM) telecommunications company, but at one point it was America's fifth largest long-distance carrier after AT&T, MCI, Sprint, and WorldCom.

Multi-level marketing was a brand-new concept to me, and I had no idea what I was getting into. When I started working with Excel, everyone told me it was a pyramid scheme, but I had no idea what they meant. I was just selling long-distance services and we were all saving money on it, so what was wrong with that?

But they were right, and the company ended up going under.

That didn't stop me, though. I joined another MLS, Fortune High-Tech Marketing (FHTM), which sold consumer goods and services. I was very successful in the first two months and built a team of forty people, but things soon started to go south. I was making "fake money," putting stuff on credit cards, and going further into debt. It was all for show, and no one was being fooled but me. Something had to change. I left FHTM, and a few years later, the Federal Trade Commission and regulators in three states shut down the company for running a pyramid scheme.

On the surface, my MLM experiences were, in a word, disastrous, but there was a huge silver lining. I started learning how to think about business, to realize that I didn't have to trade time for money just to make a living. I fell into a whole world of entrepreneur-minded individuals, go-getters who wanted to achieve more with their lives. I learned how to "fail forward," and I learned how to talk to people and network. I was in a safe space where I could dream and plan and be supported by other like-minded people. I never made any money, but the lessons I learned were worth millions.

After my failed MLM experiments, I moved around a lot, doing odd jobs here and there. I spent some time in New York City, then in Hilton Head, NC, and then moved back to Ohio. I still knew I wanted more out of life, but I lacked direction and had no clear path to making it happen.

Then in 2012, a friend called and left a cryptic voicemail: "Dude, you need to come to Cincinnati. I'm doing real estate. I'll tell you more later."

It was the message that changed my life.

CHAPTER THREE

THE 3 STRATEGIES

© 2022 www.jiriesd.com | All rights reserved

Before I get into the specific steps I took to get where I am today, I want to give you a kind of bird's eye view of the real estate landscape so that you have some context.

There are a lot of ways to make money in real estate but for most of us, they boil down to three basic strategies: Wholesaling, Flipping, and BRRRR.

In this chapter, I'll briefly go over what each strategy is and how it fit into my personal journey.

Wholesaling

Wholesaling consists of three steps:

1. A wholesaler buys a home from a seller, then
2. Finds an interested party to buy it (for a higher price than they paid), and
3. Pockets the difference as profit

As a wholesaler, I would look for and contract distressed properties. I quickly learned how to identify good properties and how to network with professionals who knew the business. A real estate wholesaler doesn't do any renovations or additions and bears no costs (unlike flipping, which we'll discuss in the next chapter).

I wholesaled because, honestly, it was great money, at least for me at that time. More importantly, though, it helped build a foundation for everything I did later. I learned to identify good deals, to tell which houses needed major repairs and which just needed minor cosmetic upgrades, and to negotiate with owners and buyers. Best of all, I was able to start with virtually no money. Trust me—you don't need millions to get started in real estate. Wholesaling is a great way to get your feet wet in the business without having to go into debt or risk your life savings.

Once I'd learned how to value a house and envision what it could look like with the right repairs, the next logical step was flipping.

Fixing-and-Flipping

I moved on to flipping houses. Unlike wholesaling, where I'd turn around and sell the property to an investor, flipping involved buying properties at reasonable prices, fixing them up, and then reselling them as residences to home buyers. There are a lot of nuances to successful flipping, which I'll discuss later, but that's the essence: Buy. Improve. Sell.

Thanks to certain reality television shows, flipping is often seen as a quick and easy way to make money. And, in fact, I did make decent money. Being able to walk away $20k or $30k richer from a single deal was a big deal for a kid who'd stood at the back of the lunch line hoping the other kids wouldn't notice how poor he was.

Eventually, though, I realized that, like wholesaling, flipping was very transactional, just a series of one-time deals. I'd put in a tremendous amount of work, but then it was done, and I'd have to keep hustling for the next big deal. It was also riskier

© 2022 www.jiriesd.com | All rights reserved

than wholesaling because much bigger sums of money were involved.

And of course, I was still trading time for money. After a while, it became exhausting. I knew there had to be more to real estate. And with the experience I had, I was ready to take the next step.

BRRRR

Hang out with real estate investors long enough, and you'll start hearing them talk about the BRRRR method. No, they're not cold; BRRRR stands for Buy, Rehab, Rent, Refinance, Repeat.

And in my opinion, it's the best way to make money in real estate.

Again, I'll get into the details on how to do this successfully later in this book. In a nutshell, though, BRRRR entails looking for properties that have the potential to increase in value, buying them, fixing them up, renting them out, refinancing them in order to pay for your next purchase, and doing that over and over again.

What I like about BRRRR is that you're not just making a quick buck; you're making monthly income from your rentals AND building a real estate portfolio that will increase in value over the long term.

It's not a get-rich-quick scheme (none of these methods are) but I've found it to be the most sustainable way to build wealth without wearing yourself out.

The Choice is Yours... but Read the Whole Book Anyway

You may be at the very beginning of your real estate journey and are reading this book simply to see what's available to you.

Or maybe you have home renovation skills, like carpentry, and can't wait to flip your first house.

Or maybe already have some money saved and are ready to jump in and buy your first rental property.

Even if you've already made up your mind to choose one strategy over the others, I encourage you to read this book in its
entirety. You don't have to go through each strategy like I did, but understanding what each one involves will help you build a firmer basis for the one(s) you choose to follow through on.

Before we do a deep dive into each strategy, though, I first want to take you through some of the "soft skills" necessary to succeed in this field. In the next chapter, we'll discuss networking and the all-important mindset.

Getting Your Real Estate Agent License

One of the things I love about real estate is that there aren't any barriers. You don't need great grades or a college education, or a certain number of years working in a specific field. It's open to anyone.

That said, I *highly* recommend investing in a real estate license. No, it's not a requirement, but it's still well worth the time and money.

Why?

1. Simply going through the process of getting your license, learning the material, and passing the exam, will give you a solid grounding in the ins and outs of the industry.

Having your license helps you understand the factors that affect the housing market, such as economic growth, interest rates, affordability of housing, the number of homes selling in the area, housing supply, new buildings, speculative demand, availability of mortgages, and number of households. It will give you a big edge over your competition.

2. Working as a realtor gives you teaches you a tremendous amount about the market. You'll learn about industry pitfalls, how to envision property, how to research neighborhoods, when to sell and when to wait, and how to negotiate.

3. You'll have an extra negotiating tactic at your fingertips: When I worked with investors who were flipping the homes they bought from me, I'd sweeten

the deal by offering to list the house at a discount, which saved them some money and brought in a little extra for myself.

4. If you can't agree with a seller on a price for a house you're trying to buy, you can at least offer to list it for them. You'll make some money, as opposed to no money, and it's still a way to meet investors and network with them.

5. And finally, you'll have an extra source of income as you build your real estate empire!

© 2022 www.jiriesd.com | All rights reserved

© 2022 www.jiriesd.com | All rights reserved

CHAPTER FOUR

MINDSET

© 2022 www.jiriesd.com | All rights reserved

Okay, I know I promised you a book about how to succeed in real estate and you're probably ready to get started and learn all the ins and outs.

But let's pause for just a moment.

Success in real estate (and, I imagine, in just about everything) isn't just about knowing the rules and following instructions. There's a whole other side to the story.

Mindset, along with the so-called "soft skills," is at least as important—maybe more important. So in this chapter, we're going to spend a few pages talking about entrepreneurship, mindset, and networking.

Entrepreneurship

I'm going to take a wild guess here: if you are reading this book, it is because you're not satisfied working 40 hours a week for someone else.

There's a joke that J.O.B. stands for Just Over Broke, meaning that while a decent job will help you pay your bills, it's very difficult to build long-term wealth with a traditional job alone.

Here's a fact: if you want to get ahead and make a decent life for yourself and your family, you're going to work hard. Do you want to work hard and build someone else's dream—or do you want to build your own?

A lot of people will hear about someone else having success in real estate and they'll think, "Huh,

© 2022 www.jiriesd.com | All rights reserved

that sounds interesting. I should learn more about that."

But only a small fraction of them will take the next step and *actually* learn more. So congratulations—simply by making the effort to read this book, you're already in a fairly elite minority.

But here's the thing: the majority of people who read this book *still* won't take action. They'll stop here, a little wiser than they were, but not any wealthier.

And that's fine. Real estate isn't for everyone, and neither is entrepreneurship.

BUT—

If you do decide to go this route, you need to develop an entrepreneurial mindset. You'll find plenty of people who can help and give you advice, but at the end of the day, it means you taking 100% responsibility for your business and your life.

That may mean a lot of hard work. You may need to do real estate on the side while you continue to work full time. When I was starting, I waited tables downtown and tended bar while I did real estate in the evenings. Work at your other job, and then dedicate three to five hours a night toward building a wholesale business. Make extra money to put aside until it is time to make a move.

It won't be easy, but it will be worth it. But you need to start thinking like an entrepreneur, not an employee, and mindset is key.

© 2022 www.jiriesd.com | All rights reserved

Mindset

There's been a lot of discussion over the past few years about "growth mindset" versus "fixed mindset." In a nutshell, the person with a growth mindset believes that they can get smarter and stronger and change their lives for the better. The fixed mindset person, on the other hand, believes that they're pretty much stuck with whatever they've got and can't do much to change anything.

The great thing is that even if you're a fixed mindset person, you can decide to be growth-minded and start making changes. You are not stuck where you are!

Our school system likes to pigeonhole us at a young age and tell us we're smart or dumb or hardworking or lazy, but the truth is that you can *decide* to be more or less of any of those qualities.

But you do have to *make* that choice.

Decide if you're not happy with where you are today. Decide if you're going to take steps to change things. Decide if you're going to stay stuck where you are, or create a whole new life for yourself and your family.

The only person who can take that first step is you.

Networking

It didn't take long once I decided to get into real estate to realize I needed help. There was only so much I could learn on my own or from the handful of people I already knew, so I started networking and getting to know people in the business.

I became good friends with my investors and the people who were buying houses for me. I spent time asking them questions and requesting their help.

And, just as importantly, I went out of my way to help *them*. I wanted to make their lives easier and provide value in any way I could, from putting lockboxes on houses for them to doing yardwork! I showed them that I was serious about learning and that I was willing to give back.

Networking is a very important step: spend time with investors and learn how they started, what mistakes they made, and how they learned their process. Go to real estate investment group (REIA) meetings and meetups. Google or meetup.com is a great place to start.

Keep the right company

Speaking of networking, start paying attention to the people you spend time with. Have you heard the phrase, "You're the average of the five people you spend the most time with"? It's true. The people you hang out with will have a huge impact on your success—or lack thereof.

If you're hanging out with fixed-mindset people who spend a lot of time complaining but never really taking action to improve their lives, it's time to find new friends. I know that sounds harsh, but those negative attitudes rub off and will bring you down.

Make a point of spending time with people who are curious and open to new ideas, who have positive attitudes, and who are taking action to improve their lives, whether through real estate or something else. These are the people who will lift you up and inspire you and ultimately contribute hugely to your success.

Know your strengths—and admit your weaknesses

Look, no one is good at everything. Maybe you've got a knack for numbers, but you suck at sales. Or maybe you absolutely love meeting new people but the deep research sends you to sleep.

That's fine. Successful real estate investing calls for a lot of different skills, and you don't have to have every single one of them. I couldn't have gotten where I am now without the help of other people. Sometimes they were people I partnered with formally. Other times, they informally helped with advice that filled the gaps in my knowledge or introduced me to people who could help.

You can do the same. Yes, you'll still have to go out and connect with people, but if you're strategic, you can look for people with strengths that complement yours and find ways to partner with them.

The Cashflow Quadrant

I didn't make the Cashflow Quadrant up; it comes from the book _Cashflow Quadrant: Rich Dad Poor Dad_ by Robert T. Kiyosaki.

It did change my life, though.

Basically, Kiyosaki says there are four "quadrants" where people make money:

E (employee)
S (small business or self-employed)
B (big business)
I (investor)

Almost all of us are taught to develop the skills that will allow us to get a job working for someone else. But Kiyosaki's point is that as long as you're trading time for dollars, you'll never achieve real financial freedom.

Becoming self-employed or starting your own business are great steps toward financial independence, but ultimately, you want to get to the "I" quadrant. And that means making your money work for you.

Real estate certainly isn't the only way of doing that, of course, but I believe it's one of the most accessible and practical. It doesn't take huge amounts of start-up capital, and it doesn't call for highly specialized knowledge or education. It's available to pretty much anyone.

If you get nothing else out of this book, I hope you'll see that financial independence doesn't have to be just a pipe dream. With the right mindset and attitude, it's available to anyone.

All right, that ends my soft skills lecture. Just remember, if you take nothing else away from this book, that success is in *your* hands, not anyone else's. You just need to make that decision and stick to it.

© 2022 www.jiriesd.com | All rights reserved

CHAPTER FIVE

WHOLESALING

"We're wholesaling real estate!" I called back the friend who'd left the mysterious message on my voice mail while I was tending bar in Hilton Head and asked him what he was talking about.

That was his answer. I had no idea what he was talking about and told him as much.

"It's okay," he reassured me. "I'll help you. It's simple. All you do is find houses that need work and sell them to real estate investors. You mark these houses up $5k–$10k, put up signs on the corners of busy shopping areas and highway exits that say, 'Handyman special, house in Forest Park, $55,000.' You put your phone number on them, and people will call you to buy these houses."

I didn't believe him. It sounded way too easy. There was no way someone would call and buy a house just because they saw a sign.

But they did. People called the numbers on those signs all the time. That was my introduction to wholesaling.

Despite not knowing much about Cincinnati, I took a chance and decided to move there. I waited tables during the day and did real estate at night, or sometimes the other way around, depending on the amount of work I was doing.

I started putting up signs all over Cincinnati, often hundreds of signs every week, and I got tons of phone calls. I sold my first house about a week after I started. I couldn't believe it.

I was hooked.

Wholesaling—a Great Intro to the Industry

Wholesaling is the process of finding a property that's undervalued, signing a contract for it, adding a reasonable fee (what's known as your "spread"), and then finding an investor to buy the contract. The investor might be buying the property as a rental or buying and flipping it; that's up to them. You are simply the middleman.

The key is that as a wholesaler, you never actually take possession of the home. You get a contract on a house, but you sell the contract to someone else—and that brings us to one of the risks, which is that you can lose the deposit ("earnest money") that you put down on a house if you can't find a buyer quickly. But if you do your research, understand what a property will be worth after it's fixed up, and only negotiate for properties that you can sell easily, you won't have to worry. (Keep reading for tips on how to evaluate a property's worth.)

Wholesaling is a great way to get your feet wet in real estate because it's quick and doesn't take much money. You can get started with as little as $500, and it's a wonderful way to learn about the industry.

To pull off a wholesale deal, you have to know what the finished product could look like and be able to assess what the home is worth and what kind of renovations it needs.

When you start wholesaling, you're going to spend a lot of time "driving for dollars," meaning that you drive around neighborhoods looking for houses that look abandoned or poorly cared for. Think high grass, weeds, piles of mail in the mailbox, etc. Then you track down the owner, make an offer, and get a contract, then turn around and sell the contract to an investor.

I wholesaled a number of houses and saved as much money as I could. After two years of being self-employed, I was able to qualify for a Veterans Administration (VA) residential bank loan and used it to buy a duplex that was in foreclosure from my own wholesale company. I fixed it up and "house-hacked," meaning I lived in one part and rented the other part out. Then I was able to get a home equity line of credit against that property, which I used to start investing in rental property.

I'll share more detail about renting in Chapter 7 and about house-hacking in Chapter 8. For now, I just want you to get a sense of how house-hacking contributed to my success.

I cannot emphasize this enough: *get your real estate license during this stage.* This is key! Having my license gave me a big edge when negotiating with sellers and agents. If I couldn't find anyone to sell to, I could still list that property for sale so I could still make some money out of it. I was then able to offer agents a discount for the listing.

After-Repair Value (ARV) and Why It's Important

Throughout this book, I'll reference ARV, the after-repair value of the property. Just like it sounds, the

ARV is what the house will be worth once it's fixed up. A good rule of thumb is that the original purchase price plus the cost of rehabbing the house should never be more than 75% of the ARV.

Is it a good investment? Use this formula. If the numbers add up to less than or equal to the ARV, it's probably a good investment. If they don't, then think again.

(Original purchase price + the cost of rehabbing the house) x .75 ≤ ARV

Let's say you're looking at a house that will be valued at $250,000 after repairs. Take that number and multiply it by 75% percent (.75). In this scenario, that's $187,000. $187,000 is your all-in maximum—in other words, the most you should spend on the purchase price *plus* repairs. Make sure you do not exceed 75% percent of the home's ARV.

But how do you figure out the ARV before you've even bought the house? The best way to figure out what a house will sell for is to research recent comparable house sales. When I say "comparable," I mean the same number of bedrooms and bathrooms, within a mile of the house you're looking at.

Zillow and Redfin are great for this, and if you can find a friendly real estate agent who can check the multiple listing service (MLS) for you, that's even better.

How Wholesalers Help

Maybe you're wondering why people would want to work with a wholesaler. Wouldn't sellers make more money and buyers save money if they cut out the middleman?

Technically, yes. However, many sellers are willing to take a lower offer because of the convenience and speed that a wholesaler offers. Sometimes you'll work with people who live out of state and have inherited a house they just want to get rid of, Other times, people need to sell quickly to avoid foreclosure, tax sale, etc. Sellers generally want a quick easy sale with a clean cash offer and no contingencies.

And what about the buyer? They don't necessarily have time to go out and look at dozens of properties. You're saving them the time and effort of looking at a lot of properties.

A good, reputable wholesaler helps bridge the gap between buyer and seller.

Becoming a Wholesale Company

After a couple of years, I decided to start my own wholesale company. My good friend Tyler has always had a knack for finding great deals, whereas I was really good at selling them—a perfect match. In 2012, we started Core Group, our own wholesale company.

As with any business, it took time to ramp up, but eventually, we had seven people working for us and were buying and selling over a hundred houses a year. We focused on helping investors new to the business buy homes, both fix-and-flip and buy-and-holds. We took the time to develop these new investors and helped educate them on what good deals look like. We'd even take them to Lowe's and Home Depot to show them what materials to use to fix up the houses before flipping them.

We had a team of people who worked well together, we kept our expenses low, and we were all making money. We focused on volume and did hundreds of wholesale transactions every single year, which was very rewarding. We were in that business for seven or eight years. I learned so much through wholesaling and, importantly, I was able to pay off my debt, and fix my credit, which made qualifying for loans much easier!

Throughout all this, I was learning the fundamentals of real estate and how to talk to investors and was becoming more credible and confident in the business, and I was able to save enough money for a down payment to buy a house of my own.

Treating Your Business Like a Business

You may be content just wholesaling a few houses a year on your own, or you may have ambitions to start your company and wholesale hundreds of properties. You can have as big or as small an operation as you like. But however, you do it—and I can't stress this enough—treat your business like a business.

> Be professional, keep records, be honest, reinvest in your business, and don't make enemies. Treat your business like a business—and it will reward you like a business.

Downsides & Moving on

As I hinted earlier, there are some downsides to the wholesale business. The main one is that as soon as you sell a house, you're unemployed again. You might make $5,000 or $10,000, which is great, but then you might not wholesale another property for another month or two.

Starting a wholesale company mitigated that to a certain extent because the sheer volume meant that we didn't have any downtime between deals. Still, I was seeing the investors we sold to make much bigger profits on the houses they bought from us, and I was ready to try something new.

I was ready to become an investor myself.

Tips:

·   Get your real estate license.
·   Treat it like a business, and it will pay you like a business.

Pros
·   Low barrier to entry. You can get started for very little
·   You'll learn how to identify a good deal vs. a bad deal
·   You'll meet other real estate investors and build your network
·   You can make some serious cash in a short amount of time—if you're willing to put in consistent work!

Cons
·   Transactional. You have to hustle constantly, which may not be sustainable in the long term
·   You can lose your earnest money if you're not careful.
·   Can be difficult to work with buyers and seller

CHAPTER SIX

FIXING & FLIPPING

As a wholesaler, I was surrounded by people who were buying houses to flip them. They would buy one house a week or as many as they wanted from me—and they were paying *cash* for these houses.

Where I was making a few thousand with each wholesale deal, these investors were making *tens* of thousands when they fixed and flipped the properties, I found for them.

I knew if they could do it, I could too, and I wanted to give it a shot.

Fixing and Flipping

Fixing and flipping means finding a house you think has potential, buying it, coming up with a budget to rehab it, and then selling it at a (hopefully large) profit.

It's a natural segue from wholesaling. You've learned how to identify good properties and negotiate for them; now you have the opportunity to make a bigger profit by taking on the investor role as well.

Unlike wholesaling, however, the barrier to entry is pretty high. You have to actually buy the house, which means at the very least you'll need enough to put down a down payment with a good lender who will give you enough money to buy and fix the house. However, the "flip" side of this method is that it is potentially much more lucrative than wholesaling.

If you are in the early stages of real estate investment, I recommend getting to know people who are doing this and working with them. They know when a house can be rehabbed, what the demo may entail, how much you should pay for finishes, what finishes go in what houses, and so on.

After-Repair Value (ARV)

A common mistake that newbie house flippers make is over-improving the property. They sink too much money into the wrong things because they think that more bells and whistles will help it sell for a higher price. But if the house is too expensive for its area, it will end up sitting on the market, costing the investor money for every day that it doesn't sell. Don't splurge on marble countertops in a Formica countertop neighborhood, for example, and always see if you can refinish something instead of outright replacing it.

Research similar properties in the area to determine the fair market value for the house you're flipping, and then plan your repairs and renovations to improve the property to that point or even slightly better. Of course, it should look nice and meet codes, but don't go overboard—an expensive house in a middle-of-the-road neighborhood is likely to just sit there for months with no offers and eventually sell for less than you'd hoped.

What I learned from my fixing-and-flipping days is that flipping *can* be lucrative, but for me, ultimately, it wasn't worth it. It was riskier because I was dealing with much bigger sums of money than with wholesaling, but it was also transactional, meaning that there was no potential for long-term appreciation and wealth-building.

Also bear in mind that you're dealing with a longer timeline than you would in wholesaling. On average, it takes eight to nine months from the day you buy to the day you sell, and the longer it takes, the more it costs you in taxes, interest, and utilities.

And don't forget that you have to depend on contractors and hope that they're reliable and able to work on your schedule.

And once you sell your house, you're unemployed and you have to find another one and start all over again at square one.

I learned a lot from flipping, so I don't regret it, but if I had to skip one step of my journey, it would probably be this one.

In the next chapter, I'll share my journey from flipping to the next step: Buying, Rehabbing, Renting, Refinancing, and Repeating.

Tips, Pros, and Cons of the Fix and Flip Method

Tips
· Get connected and talk to other people in your area who are investing.
· Get involved if you can; if you can't, find someone you TRUST who can manage the job and stay on them. Check in at least every other day.
· Don't bite off more than you can chew. Some of the best deals you'll do are the ones you don't.
· Educate yourself!

Pros
· Solid asset that you can touch and see.
· Great opportunity to make a big chunk of cash
· Can be a good way to raise capital

Cons
· Very transactional; you have to be constantly on the lookout for properties
· Dealing with realtors and buyers
· Chance of having to deal with a problem you didn't see when you bought it
· Missing out on the property's appreciation and rental "cash cow"
·

CHAPTER SEVEN

BRRRR

© 2022 www.jiriesd.com | All rights reserved

One day, I called my friend Nate, someone I've always looked up to. He's another busy (or so I thought) real estate investor and I called to get his advice about some deal I was working on. It was about 11 a.m. on a weekday, and I asked him what he was up to.

"Just out sledding with my kids," he replied.

What?! How could this guy be taking the morning off? "Don't you have work to do?" I asked him.

"Nah," he said. "I already made a million dollars this year. Why should I keep hustling when I can spend time with my kids?"

I'd always known that Nate owned a lot of units, but I'd never taken the time to really think about what that meant. I was doing well with wholesaling and flipping, but it suddenly occurred to me that I could never stop. As long as I wanted income, I'd have to keep hustling. Once I sold a house, it was gone—I no longer had a way to make more money from it.

I wanted to step back from having to hustle all the time and instead create passive income and focus on building wealth.

Investing in rental properties seemed like the next logical step, but one of the first things I learned—the hard way—was that building wealth through rental properties is *not* just about rent.

But before I started buying anything, I fixed my credit. This is a very important first step. If you have bad credit, make it good. If you have good credit, make it great.

Next, I found a distressed house we were going to wholesale, but I ended up buying it for myself as a primary residence, using a Veteran's Administrative (VA) loan to buy it for $145,000. I put about $110,000 into the house. When it was all said and done, it appraised for $360K.

Because of that, I was able to get a credit line against my house for $130,000. And that's how I started to buy my first rental properties—by using a credit line on my house.

The Cash Cow vs. the Golden Goose

The first rental property I bought was a three-bedroom, one-bath ranch slab in a Cincinnati neighborhood called Colerain. It was a great price, and I knew I could get a decent rental income from it, and I snapped it up as soon as I found it.

I was telling my friend Nate how excited I was when he threw a wet blanket all over my shiny plans. I'll never forget his words: "Dude, you can't buy that."

"Why? What's wrong with it?" I asked. "It's nice, and I picked it up for $60,000. Anyway, I already bought it, so it's too late."

"That house is worth $100,000 max today," Nate explained patiently. "Even if you put $80,000 into rehabbing it, a year from now, it's going to be worth $100,000. Four years from now, it'll be worth a little more just because of appreciation, but it still probably won't be worth $180,000. But another house in another neighborhood might be worth double that."

© 2022 www.jiriesd.com | All rights reserved

I found it hard to believe there was no upside to buying property in that area. But he was right.

Rental income is a cash cow. It's good, consistent money, and that's great. And if you have five or six properties, it can be a very respectable side income. But most of us won't be able to actually live off rental income alone until we have thirty or forty rental properties because the majority of rental income will be going to pay off loans.

However, if you're smart about the properties you buy, you can reap the benefits of them appreciating in value. Property appreciation is your golden goose. It helps you build serious wealth without doing any extra work.

Imagine buying a property that increases in value from $100,000 to $200,000 over the course of seven years. If that happens with five or six properties, you've just made hundreds of thousands of dollars simply by owning those properties.

Nate stressed the importance of thinking about long-term value. The key, he explained, was research. "You've got to look into what's going on in the city," he said. "You've got to be in the city, and you've got to see what's going on."

Best advice ever!

Researching Rentals

I followed Nate's advice and began looking at what was going on in the city. I started researching what neighborhoods would be good *in the future*—

and that didn't necessarily mean they were always good now.

Before you invest in a particular property, take the time to study the neighborhood. What zoning is changing? What is being discussed in city council meetings? Where are the new coffee shops popping up? I learned to do a ton of research about any area I was thinking about investing in.

And it paid off.

I read papers and bought business journals and took the time to learn about what was happening in my city. One major headline popped up explaining that the mayor had approved funds to build an on-ramp from the interstate to the Incline District. The Incline District of East Price Hill, a neighborhood in Cincinnati, rests on top of the western section of the former Price Hill Incline. The area had been in decline for many years, but there were many hidden jewels, including Italianate row houses, Shingle and Queen Anne Victorians, and Colonials.

It was tough to see how the area could become a thriving designated entertainment zone. But more research revealed that a non-profit community development organization was making serious strides in revitalizing the area and that new restaurants and coffee shops were opening.

It was starting to look promising.

While I was in the Price Hill area looking around and talking to people, somebody approached me about buying a building on Mt. Hope, the main street there. After doing my due diligence, I ended up buying a three-unit building.

When I was done rehabbing it, the property appraised for $135,000. Today, five years later, it's worth $400,000.

Get to know your city! Do research and know where things are happening in your city. Factors such as good schools, job proximity, and retail and recreational options will support the long-term appeal for tenants—and for buyers when it comes time to sell.

Research Tips

Key areas to research:
· Location
· Construction
· Market
· Job Growth

How to research:
· Read the local and state papers
· Attend city council meetings
· Go to neighborhood meetings
· Join neighborhood groups on social media

Strategies for long-term success—and sanity

My strategy became: buy a home, renovate it, find a tenant, refinance, and get my money back. I got to the point that I was wholesaling houses from my wholesale company to my real estate company because they were good deals.

I have a few single-family rentals, but I focus mainly on two-, three-, and four-unit buildings, which allows for economies of scale. Since the point of this is to build passive income, it pays to set yourself up so that you're not constantly dealing with complaints and repairs.

Unlike flipping, where you don't want to over-improve a property, it's smart to over-improve your rental properties. This is because you're investing in neighborhoods that are on the upswing (right?!) so your properties need to be in line with future expectations. When I rehab my rentals, I use high-quality materials and equipment that won't need ongoing upkeep and repair. This helps maintain the home's value and saves me the headache of dealing with complaints from my tenants.

I also screen tenants carefully because I want quality renters who will treat the property with respect and who will be easy and pleasant to work with. Address any issues that come up immediately and make sure you have a paper trail of all communication and transactions.

Another bit of sanity-saving advice: create systems so that you're not reinventing the wheel with each new property. From the moment you start, keep notes on what works and what doesn't. Use those notes to create a manual that you can share with people who work for you so that everyone knows exactly what steps to take when.

We've now covered the basics of wholesaling, flipping and BRRRR, but no book on real estate

Residential or Commercial—Know Your Options

Residential real estate can include single-family homes, townhomes, condos, mobile homes, and multiplex buildings and is zoned accordingly.

Commercial real estate is a property that is rented to a business rather than an individual for personal use. It can include apartment complexes, hotels, industrial spaces, retail spaces, and office spaces.

investing would be complete without a discussion on financing. After all, you've got to come up with the money to buy the properties that will build your wealth, right?

In the next chapter, I'll explain the various financing methods and discuss which ones might be right for you.

© 2022 www.jiriesd.com | All rights reserved

CHAPTER EIGHT

FINANCING

I cannot emphasize enough the importance of finding a worthwhile property—but the right property is only one part of the equation.

Unless you happen to have a boatload of cash lying around—and frankly, even if you *do* have a boatload of cash lying around—you'll want to find financing, and the *right* financing will be critical to your overall success.

There are real estate financing options available to fund every type of investment. It pays to understand your options because the method by which a specific deal is funded can greatly impact its outcome.

In this chapter, we'll walk through the various types of financing so you can find the one that best suits your needs. You can also find a free resource on our website, JiriesD.com.

Successful financing is simply a matter of being knowledgeable about what strategies exist and leveraging them properly. When in doubt, use your network and ask the experts you know for advice and connections.

DSCR—Your Key to Success

When investing in real estate, you'll want to work with a debt-service coverage ratio (DSCR) lender, which is simply a financial institution that awards investors loans that are repaid using the income from the property to be purchased or refinanced. These loans use a formula to qualify the loans and validate whether the property will generate sufficient cash flow to cover the monthly debt payments.

In the context of business finance, such as real estate investing, DSCR is a measurement of a firm's available cash flow to pay current debt obligations. The DSCR helps investors determine whether a company has enough income to pay its debts. DSCR is also used to analyze firms, projects, and individual borrowers.

The formula itself is straightforward:

Take the monthly gross projected rental income as determined based on an existing lease agreement or an appraiser's opinion of market value rent.

Then divide that operating income by the total, the monthly amount of the loan payments.

If the resulting quotient is 1.0, the ratio of income to debt is break-even.

A quotient greater than 1.0 indicates positive cash flow after the debt is serviced.

The minimum DSCR that a lender demands depends on many conditions. A DSCR above 1.25 is often considered "strong," whereas ratios below 1.00 could indicate that the company (or person) is facing financial difficulties. A DSCR loan may still be possible even with a quotient less than 1.0, provided there are other assets and income sources to cover any potential issues.

Note the items that contribute to calculating DSCR value can include but are not limited to: gross monthly rent, property taxes, insurance, vacancy %, HOA Fees, and property management fees.

Why DSCR?

DSCR loans are attractive for a number of reasons. First, the ability to repay is based on income from the property as opposed to employment income (as with a regular mortgage), so these loans work for investors who don't necessarily get a steady paycheck, like business owners, the self-employed, and retirees.

For the same reason, first-time investors don't have to demonstrate a track record with income-generating properties. Note that it's not uncommon to pay more in points or origination fees on your first DSCR loan with a new lender. But as the relationship develops, so will their trust and your costs should decrease as time progresses.

DSCR loans may be used to finance properties featuring short or long-term rentals, so they're an option if you're thinking about going the Airbnb route, not just the traditional rental route.

Important Notes About DSCR Loans

DSCR loans are not typically run through conventional banks, so you will need to find your lenders online or get referrals from your network. Some lenders may give you a loan if your credit score is as low as 650, but for the best rates, try to get it to 707 or above.

To qualify for a DSCR loan, you must have an LLC or other type of registered company. Since DSCR loans are in your company's name, they won't affect your personal credit score (except possibly for the initial pull to confirm your credit worthiness), unless you default. By not reporting to your personal credit report, it will benefit the debt-to-income ratio on your personal spending.

Depending upon your experience and the deal, the lender will likely require reserves set aside for at least two to six months prior to close. Find out what their criteria are to minimize any surprises.

Typically, DSCR lenders may be a bit more expensive than traditional bank loans. Closing costs will typically be higher as well as the lender may look to escrow or impound several months' worth of taxes and insurance.

Sometimes a good DSCR lender can also help you buy the property as a fixer-upper if you need to. It is certainly worth investigating all possibilities with a DSCR lender as you move forward in the very important step.

Self-Directed IRA (Individual Retirement Account)

As of this writing in 2022, inflation is at an all-time high. People with money in IRAs are getting terrible returns and even losing money. Even if they're making 10% interest, inflation is at 7½ % so the actual return is only 2½%.

Based on where we are today with inflation, leveraging a self-directed IRA (Individual Retirement Account) may be a great way to provide flexibility and improve cash flow. A self-directed IRA at its most basic level is a savings account that allows for compounded, tax-free growth over time. The owner of the IRA still very much has control of various investment options, including real estate. Self-directed IRAs are unique from other savings accounts, such as a 401K, but check with your financial advisor.

Owners of self-directed IRA accounts enjoy the unique benefit of purchasing, rehabbing, and selling properties while still being able to defer taxes. However, it is important to note that owners under 60 are typically subject to a penalty for withdrawing funds early.

Please remember: when using funds from your self-directed IRA, you must follow the IRA's rules carefully. It's certainly doable, but there may be extra hoops to jump through or steps to implement in your process to ensure you're doing it properly. I strongly encourage you to educate yourself properly if you're planning on using funds from a self-directed IRA to build your portfolio.

Cash Financing

This is a great option for investors who have access to a significant amount of capital, either personally or through their network, and wish to purchase properties free and clear.

As an investor, cash is a huge tool for getting what you want. You can close more quickly, which helps you get more offers accepted. Cash financing also enables investors to save on interest, increase their cash flow, and receive instant equity in their investments.

There will be times when paying cash for property makes sense and other times when other financing options should be considered. However, if you have your own capital, you should always consider using it in the best possible scenarios. Just remember to not spread yourself too thin, and if you can use Other People's Money (OPM), do it. The cash reserves will look great to them and show that you're responsible with money.

Private Money Lenders

Private money means working with our family or friends. They may want to invest their money somewhere, so why not with you?

Networking is key—you may know investors who are well-connected and can often tap into capital from personal connections, borrowing money at a specified interest rate and payback period. Private money lenders are integral to the growth of every new investor. They have the means and intent to invest capital into your business, and they are just as interested in working with you as you are with them.

Generally speaking, private money lenders will provide investors with cash to purchase real estate properties in exchange for a specific interest rate. You can offer security to the lender by showing their note has interest in the property until settled. These terms will generally be established upfront and with a specified payback period, usually anywhere from six months to a year.

These loans are most common when investors believe they can raise the value of a particular property over a short period of time, typically through renovations. It's also important to understand that private money should only be used when you have a clearly defined exit strategy like hard money. This makes it a good choice when flipping.

A great way to promote this is through social media. You don't necessarily have to post that you are looking for investors, just let people know what you are doing. Let people see the houses you're doing even if you've only done one deal, even if you're working on your first one. Every single day, post something about the work you're doing. This piques people's interest and some will almost always ask if you are looking for possible partners and investors.

Hard Money Lenders

Hard money lenders make short-term loans available to investors who have less-than-perfect credit or financial history.

Funded by private businesses and individuals, hard money lenders provide short-term, high-interest-rate loans for real estate investors. This particular option is often used by flippers.

The way hard money financing is configured, you use the value of the investment property itself, with lenders analyzing the "After Repair Value" (ARV) to determine the size of the loan. Hard money lenders won't usually fund an entire deal but rather a percentage of the purchase price or the after-repair value, ranging from 50% to 70%.

Hard money lenders also charge fees apart from the interest on the loan. These fees are generally delineated in points (three to five), representing additional percentage fees based on the loan amount. In general, hard money lenders charge much higher interest rates—sometimes double the amount of a traditional mortgage, plus fees.

Different hard money lenders have different requirements, and real estate investors need to be fully aware of what they're getting themselves into.

A hard money lender is going to be typically more expensive than a private investor, probably between 9% and 30%. But they'll also be very easy to work with. Find one who is focused on real estate and cares about property. They will help you get to the finish line, whether you are flipping the property to sell it or keeping it as a rental.

Seller Financing

Seller financing is a great way to get a property with essentially no money down/nothing out of pocket, can help sellers push back capital gains

© 2022 www.jiriesd.com | All rights reserved

Often, buyers and sellers work together to avoid private lenders altogether. In seller financing, the property buyer will make payments directly to the seller of the property rather than going through a bank. This can help a motivated seller sell the property more quickly, and the investor can avoid jumping over traditional mortgage-lending hurdles, such as credit score minimums.

Together, the buyer and seller can often enjoy a faster transaction process and avoid many costs and fees associated with the closing process. Furthermore, the seller can sell the promissory note if they no longer want to manage their own owner financing. Another benefit to seller financing is that if the seller owns it free and clear, it is a way for them to offset their capital gains.

You may also be able to secure owner financing through lease options, wrap-around mortgages, and subject-to. A great alternative financing option, a subject-to-mortgage can tip the scale in buyers' favor, but only when carried out responsibly and with the proper knowledge of how to proceed. In a nutshell, it involves the buyer taking over the seller's mortgage payments while leaving the existing mortgage in place, with a contract that gives the investor the right to sell the property. If the seller is facing foreclosure, it can benefit their credit. The investor, meanwhile, can avoid closing costs, origination fees, and other costs, which means more room for profit down the line.

Seller financing overlaps with a number of different strategies and could be a book in itself. We don't have time to cover it in detail here; just remember that seller financing is an out-of-the-box approach that can be a powerful tool when done properly.

Peer-To-Peer Lending

This is a great option for investors trying to raise the last portion of funding for a project. Peer-to-peer lending offers high flexibility and low interest rates.

Peer-to-peer lending allows investors to borrow money from other investors or groups of investors (hence the name). The basic process is similar to hard or private money lending, though the specifics are quite different. Like these methods, investors can bypass traditional funding requirements and allow their portfolios to do the talking.

But this form of real estate financing typically involves a lower loan-to-value ratio than other funding types. This could prevent investors from borrowing the entire loan amount needed to purchase a property. Again, ask—talk to people and look into the financing you need. This option may offer a lot of flexibility overall.

House-Hacking

House-hacking isn't a form of financing, per se. It's a way of using your residential property (i.e., your own home) to generate income for investment purposes.

Let's say you've picked up this book because you want to get into real estate investing and have no idea where to begin. Financing seems overwhelming, and the plethora of options can be staggering.

So, let's start slowly...

House-hacking is a great option to get started in real estate investing with very little money down. Because you're buying a home to live in yourself, you qualify for owner-occupied financing, which means low interest rates and low down payments.

Multifamily properties are the classic model for house-hacking: you buy a multifamily property, move into one of the units, and rent out the other(s). Your neighboring tenants pay you rent every month, and their rent covers your mortgage payment.

In my experience, this works best when you buy something with four units or less. Properties with up to four units are classified as "residential" in the US, so you can take out a traditional mortgage to buy one and still qualify as an owner-occupant. For house-hacking to be a benefit, you want to buy as an owner-occupant, because you can get an FHA loan and put down as little as 3% on that property.

Using a four-unit as an example, if the lender will allow you to count 75% of the rental income available, this could be derived from the three units that you are renting. Therefore, the fourth unit you are house-hacking is not considered. That allows you to buy an investment property with only 3% down, live in one unit, and rent out the other three units.

You're basically getting paid to own a house while putting down only 3%.

Not only can tenants' rent cover an entire mortgage, but there's also money left over each month to put towards repairs, vacancy rate, and other rental-related expenses.

You can also tap into the Airbnb industry for short-term leases and potentially obtain higher returns.

Perhaps you prefer a single-family home or live in one already. There is no need to move out of your current home. You can rent a second bedroom or a lower level to housemates. College-style living is a great example of this.

> While these are great options for a lower down payment, make sure you investigate every possible detail before signing over to a renter.

How to Make a Million with 3% Down

Using one of the house-hack financing options, buy a duplex for $380,000, putting $11,400 (3%) down. Assuming a 30-year mortgage rate of 7.76% (the current rate as of this writing), your monthly mortgage payments will be $2641.

© 2022 www.jiriesd.com | All rights reserved

Live in one unit and rent the other out for $2700 a month.

Wait 30 years (and assume a 3.5% appreciation rate).

Your home is paid off and worth $1,000,0000. Congratulations!

Okay, that's a *little* bit simplified—how much you can make in rent depends on a lot of different factors, and we haven't taken taxes and insurance into consideration. But it lets you see how you can turn your original investment of $11,400 into a heck of a lot more doing something you were probably going to do (buy a house) anyway.

House-Hack Financing

Because you'll be living on the property, you should consider residential loans offered by the government, traditional lenders, and methods of leveraging personal equity.

FHA Loan: The Federal Housing Administration (FHA) loan is one of several home loan options offered by the federal government. The FHA established the loan to help broaden access to homeownership for consumers with less-than-perfect credit profiles and those who do not have the financial means to save up for a large down payment. When a new homebuyer shops for mortgage loan options, they can search for lenders that offer mortgage loan products backed by the FHA. These loans offer a down payment requirement of as low as 3.5% while still giving a low interest rate.

However, it should be noted that putting down less than 20% on a home loan will result in a required private mortgage insurance payment (PMI). Also, the FHA loan only covers owner-occupied properties but does allow for purchasing a property with more than one unit.

According to The Lenders Network, the current loan limit for a single-unit property ranges between $294,515 to $679,650, depending on whether the market is a low-cost or high-cost area.

Traditional Mortgage Loan: A conventional home loan is a very popular method of financing real estate deals. These are typically financed by banks. This has been a popular method of financing in recent years because interest rates have been at historic lows—although they are rising as I write this.

One thing to note: traditional lenders follow tight guidelines with many demands that other financing options don't require. The hurdles include a sufficient down payment (anywhere from 15% to 25%), an adequate credit score (a minimum of 680), and documentation of income. Also, the money used must be called "sourced and seasoned," meaning that funds must be traceable and have been in your account for 30 to 90 days, and they cannot be a gift. This could limit many investors.

VA Loan: A VA loan is a mortgage guaranteed by the United States Department of Veterans Affairs.

VA loans are intended to service United States veterans, service members, and their spouses. They are issued by qualified lenders and guaranteed by the U.S. Department of Veterans Affairs (VA). Specifically, the VA will guarantee a maximum of 25% of a home loan amount up to $113,275, which limits the maximum loan amount to $453,100. According to VAloans.com, "You may generally borrow up to the reasonable value of the property or the purchase price, whichever is less, plus the funding fee, if required."

Home Equity Loan: A home equity loan, more formally known as a Home Equity Line of Credit (HELOC), allows homeowners to leverage their home equity as collateral to take out a loan. Common uses for home equity loans include home repairs, education, or resolving debt.

When you have built up equity in your personal residence, either through principal reduction and/or appreciation, you may have the opportunity to take out a home equity loan.

Benefits of home equity loans are that they are interest-only and the low rates are typically based on the prime rate. The interest is only paid on the amount that is taken out, not the full amount available. Also, borrowers enjoy the flexibility to use the loan to manage their own repayment structure.

This flexibility creates an avenue for homeowners to expand their portfolios on their own terms.

Which Financing Option Should You Choose?
Remember the **_BRRRR_** method: Buy, Rehab, Rent, Refinance, REPEAT. Financing is necessary for the Buy and Refinance steps and is therefore a critical part of your success. Take the time to do your homework. It's helpful to focus on your long-term goals and preferred investment strategy.

For example, if you plan on using real estate as a way to bolster your retirement savings, it may be smart to think about using an IRA. On the other hand, if your long-term goal is to have your own real estate investing business, then options like a hard money lender may be a better fit.

Another consideration when choosing a financing option is what type of real estate strategy you're pursuing, as some financing options may be better suited for different investment types. Many investors find that a home equity loan can help finance a rental property, while private money lenders may be what you need for a rehab property.

Think through why you are investing in real estate and weigh the pros and cons of each option before deciding how to finance it.

© 2022 www.jiriesd.com | All rights reserved   69

CHAPTER NINE

BUILDING THE DREAM TEAM

Nothing great is achieved alone. No single person has the expertise, energy, or time to do it all on their own. Whether you're wholesaling, flipping, renting, or some combination, you're going to need help.

Surrounding yourself with a strong team will make your life easier, make your transactions smoother, and will take years off your journey to success. It will take time to find the right people and build relationships with them, but that time is one of the best investments you can make.

Following are the people I consider absolutely essential to every real estate investor's team:

Realtor
If you're not a realtor yourself, find one who is investor-friendly. They can help you pull comps, get you into showings, and obtain data on houses the minute they hit the market. Even if you're a realtor yourself, take the time to get to know other realtors in your area. They're a rich source of information and advice.

Real Estate Attorney
A good real estate lawyer will help you out with contracts, lease options, evictions and more, and can advise you in knowing what you and cannot do legally in your specific state and city.

Be sure to find an attorney who specializes in real estate.

Title Company

A title company helps close transactions, making sure there are no liens, restrictions, or encumbrances against the deed. You'll almost certainly be dealing with less traditional financing, such as seller financing, subject-to, and promissory notes, so look for one that's investor friendly and that has experience in working with people like you.

Mentor

I can't tell you how valuable it was for me to surround myself with people who were at a higher level than I was. A good mentor is like a cheat sheet to success and is arguably the most important member of your team.

Finding people who can answer your questions is great, but finding someone who is willing to push you and challenge you as well is even better. A good mentor will help you grow as both an investor and as a person.

Seek out people who have had the results that you want and build relationships with them. And don't take them for granted! Make yourself indispensable to them by helping them wherever

© 2022 www.jiriesd.com | All rights reserved

you can, and always tell them how much you appreciate them.

Other Steps

I suggest creating a business entity to house your real estate endeavors. This decreases your personal exposure, gives you access to certain types of funding, and makes you look more professional.

A limited liability company (LLC) is usually the easiest to create, but there are others that may suit your particular situation better. I suggest talking to a lawyer who specializes in helping small businesses.

While you're at it, take a little time to establish a brand. Get a logo, a website, and marketing material (check out Fiverr for affordable options). Again, you'll look more professional and people will take you more seriously.

And don't forget to treat your business like a business. That means dressing well when meeting with sellers and investors, answering the phone when leads call you, and being available as much as possible.

The more you put into it, the more you'll get out.

Investing is not for the faint of heart. Many times, it may be tempting to retreat back to a traditional job. However, if you commit to learning the ropes, your anxiety will start to settle and you will be on your way to being a real estate investor.

Real estate doesn't care about your GPA, your race, your ethnic background, or your gender. If you put in the work, if you know your numbers, and if you follow the steps outlined in this book, you'll do well.

And if you want more support or a deeper understanding of how it all works, we can help you through this process. Considering how much the market changes, we have put a free resource on our website to help you with the elements you have learned throughout this book.

You can also sign up for videos and/or coaching at our site: **www.jiriesd.com**

NOTES

ACKNOWLEGEMENTS

A huge thank you to my parents for instilling in me a great work ethic and tolerating me through all the ups and downs of the lessons I learned in this book.

To my friends who have always had my back over the years, thank you.

To Tyler Parker. I wouldn't be where I'm at today if it wasn't for having one of the best friends and business partners I could ever ask for. Together, we were able to build many successful companies from wholesaling to buying rental properties. I am excited to see what the future holds for both of us!

Thank you to Nate Barger and Mike Ealy for helping me out and being there to answer my many questions. You helped me on my journey from buying a single-family home to buying hotels. Two years ago, I never even knew you could franchise a hotel. Nate and Mike, you both opened my eyes to incredible possibilities. You were an integral part of my journey from selling residential to commercial real estate to being a hotel investor.

Jes and Gabe, thank you for always putting up with my crazy ideas! You two motivate me to improve and learn every single day.

Thank you all from the bottom of my heart.

© 2022 www.jiriesd.com | All rights reserved

ABOUT JIRIES DAWAHER

Jiries Dawaher came from a large immigrant family whose work ethic was paramount in his upbringing. After several attempts at various careers, one finally struck a chord—real estate. A serious setback in his life almost kept him from taking the next step. But he took a risk and jumped all in on real estate. His journey was tough, but he persevered and now shares the keys to his multi-million dollar success with people all over America.

For more information, please contact Jiries through his website: jiriesd.com

www.ingramcontent.com/pod-product-compliance
Lightning Source LLC
Chambersburg PA
CBHW022049190326
41520CB00008B/755